HAL LEONARD
GUITAR METHOD
Supplement to Any Guitar Method

BRAZILIAN GUITAR

BY CARLOS ARANA

T0039765

PLAYBACK+
Speed • Pitch • Balance • Loop

To access audio visit:
www.halleonard.com/mylibrary
Enter Code
3759-9283-0953-0034

ISBN 978-1-4584-0276-9

HAL•LEONARD®
7777 W. BLUEMOUND RD. P.O. BOX 13819 MILWAUKEE, WI 53213

Visit Hal Leonard Online at
www.halleonard.com

CONTENTS

INTRODUCTION

Brazilian music is well-known among music lovers for its rich, sophisticated sound. When played on guitar, one of the most ubiquitous instruments in Brazil's music universe, it requires control over each and every aspect and variable of the instrument. Thus different approaches are needed to assimilate and later play this music.

This book provides insight into these approaches. Inside you will find the techniques, resources, and the terminology of Brazilian guitar, all shown through the most popular songs of the Brazilian repertoire. Some of the songs are transcribed note-for-note and played in their most popular versions. Others are adapted (or transcribed from one of the hundreds of versions available) for the specific topic that I will address within the general educational focus.

To take full advantage of this book, the readers should be familiar with rhythm reading, four-part harmony, and the basis of functional harmony. Otherwise, in my book *Bossa Nova Guitar* (Hal Leonard), readers can find these concepts explained in detail for a better understanding of the basic references required for approaching Brazilian guitar.

Remember that learning about music requires both practice and experience. I recommend that you become familiar with as much material as you can find about Brazilian guitar and learn about its most emblematic performers, as these are the people who gave and continue to give this marvelous genre its prestige, beauty, and sophistication.

CHAPTER 1: PRELIMINARY CONCEPTS

RHYTHM PATTERNS

As with all Latin American music, in the different rhythms of Brazilian music, the guitar player's right hand imitates the percussion instruments that make up its typical ensemble. Thus we must get to know the most important rhythmic aspects of Brazilian music in general before examining each genre more closely. These include the following:

- Played in 2/4 time

- Basic subdivision is the 16th note

- Constant syncopation

Rhythm Figures Using Eighth and Sixteenth Notes

The seven rhythm figures (or cells) below are essential in all of the Brazilian rhythms that we will study in this book. Musicians should thus be able to play them all in a natural, precise way in order to get the flavor typical of these rhythms.

I will present them in cells that are each one quarter note long. As we saw above, since most songs have time signatures of 2/4, if we put two of them together, we will get a full bar.

The seven basic rhythm cells are:

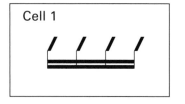

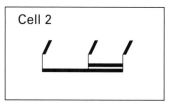

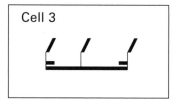

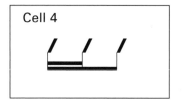

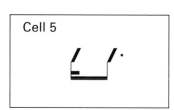

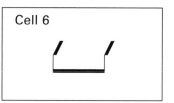

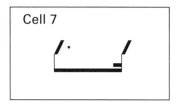

As a training exercise on these cells, I propose combining them. The best way to do this is to mark the beat (the quarter note in the 2/4 bar) with the thumb (and foot) and the cells with the *i-m-r* block—i.e., the index, middle, and ring fingers of the right hand. For now, just use any chord for these examples.

Here are a few of the possible combinations:

Same Rhythmic Cell (Cell 2)

Two Different Cells (Cell 3 and Cell 6)

Syncopation

Syncopation refers to the stressing of a weak beat or a weak part of a beat. We can create different types of syncopation by connecting (with a tie) the last sixteenth note of each cell to the first one in the next cell. This creates numerous patterns, which, as we will see, are very typical of Brazilian rhythms.

Now let's see the same examples from before with syncopation:

Same Rhythmic Cells (Cell 2)

Two Different Cells (Cell 3 and Cell 6)

CHORDS

Another essential factor in Brazilian guitar is the harmony. All types of chords are used, from simple triads to chords with four voices or more, and they're often loaded with tensions.

Presented below are the chord shapes most commonly used in these rhythms. First we'll look at slash chords, or chords in which the bass note is different than the root, and then we'll look at some chords with tensions. (Though there are many slash chords possible, all the ones shown here are inversions—i.e., a chord in which a tone other than the root is in the bass.) I would like to clarify that this is only a sample of the harmonic vocabulary used in Brazilian guitar. I highly recommend further study in this regard, as this topic has been thoroughly covered in many other publications.

Inverted Chords

- ■   Bass
- ●   Root
- ○   Chord tone, extension, or alteration

Major Chords

- 1st Inversion (bass is major 3rd of the chord)

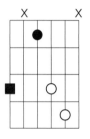 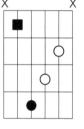 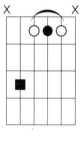 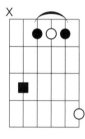 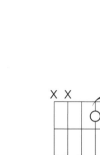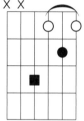

- 2nd Inversion (bass is perfect 5th of the chord)

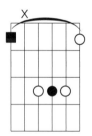 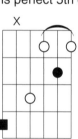 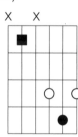 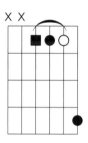 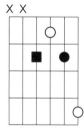

Minor Chords

- 1st Inversion (bass is minor 3rd of the chord)

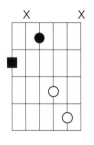 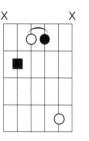 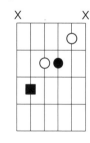 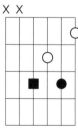 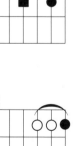

- 2nd Inversion (bass is perfect 5th of the chord)

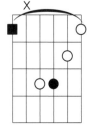 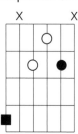 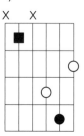 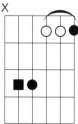

Seventh Chords

• 1st Inversion (bass is major 3rd of the chord)

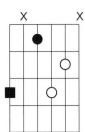 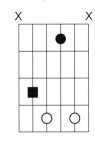 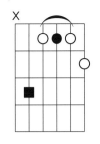 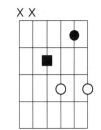

• 2nd Inversion (bass is perfect 5th of the chord)

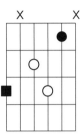 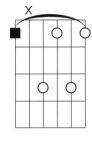 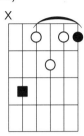 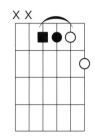

• 3rd Inversion (bass is minor 7th of the chord)

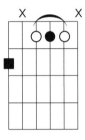 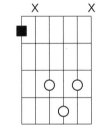 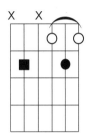 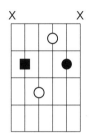

Sixth Chords

• Sixth Chord, 1st Inversion (bass is major 3rd of the chord)

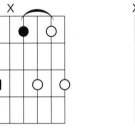 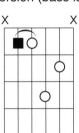

• Minor Sixth Chord, 1st Inversion (bass is minor 3rd of the chord)

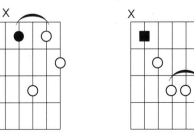

Chords with Extensions and Alterations

Major Chords

• maj7

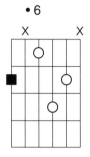 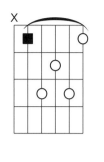 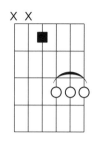 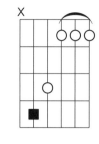

• 6

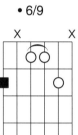 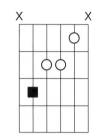 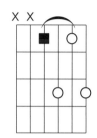

• 6/9

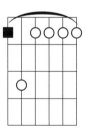 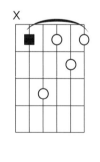 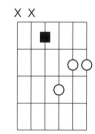

Minor Chords

• m7

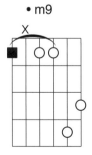 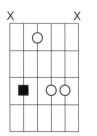 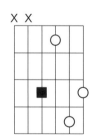 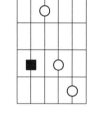

• m9

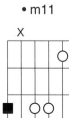 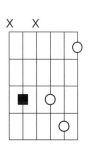 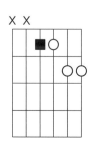

• m11

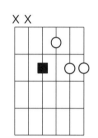 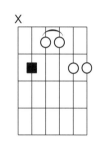 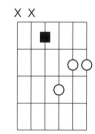

Minor Chords (continued)

• m6

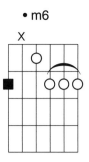 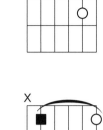 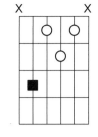

• m(maj7)

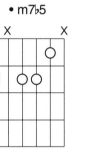 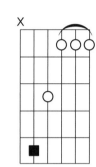 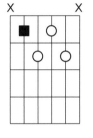 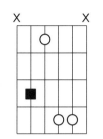

• m7♭5

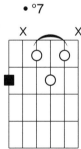 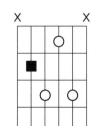 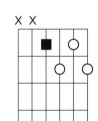 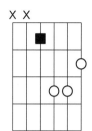

Diminished and Augmented Chords

• °7

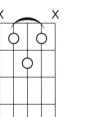 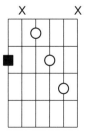 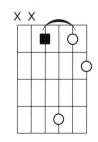

• °7♭13

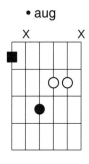 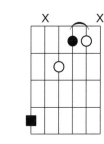 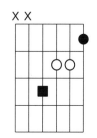

• aug

Dominant Chords

• 7

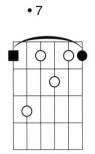 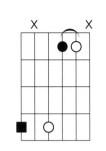 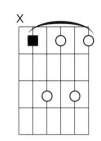 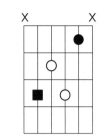

• 9

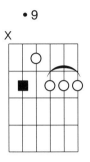 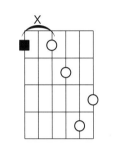 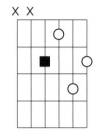 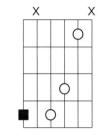

• 13

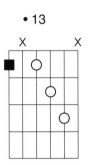 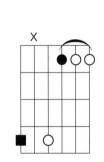 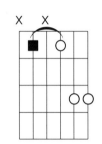

• 7sus4

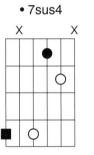 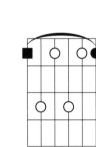 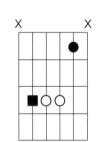

• 9sus4

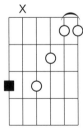 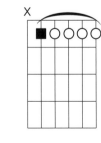 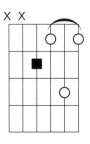

• 7♭9

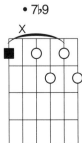 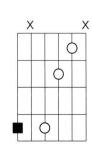 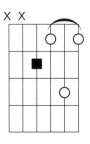 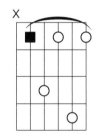

Dominant Chords (continued)

• 7♯9 and 7♯9♯5

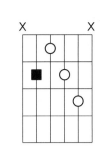 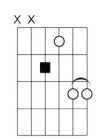 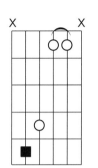 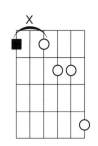

• 7♭5 or 7♯11

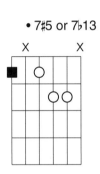 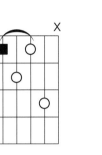 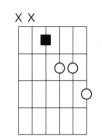 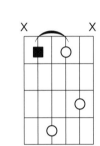

• 7♯5 or 7♭13

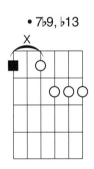

• 7♭9, ♭13

CHAPTER 2: SAMBA, CHORO, AND BOSSA NOVA

I present these three styles together because they were all born and developed in Rio de Janeiro, and they are all closely related. In fact, you'll often hear of two common sub-genres: the *choro-samba* and the *samba-bossa nova*.

The *carioca* rhythms (*carioca* is the term used to refer to Rio de Janeiro and its inhabitants) are those that represent Brazil throughout the world, and the reason is clear; for many years, Rio de Janeiro was the capital of Brazil, and though that's changed, it continues to be the cultural and artistic capital of the country. This applies not only in terms of music, but in all expressions of art. For this reason, we will begin by studying these genres because they are the ones that will allow us to study and understand the rhythms of other regions of Brazil.

To begin, we will analyze *choro* and *samba*. Although the moment at which both of these rhythms originated is not entirely clear, it is safe to say that both were born in Rio de Janeiro because of the recordings that survive to this day and the artists that made them famous. Thus samba and choro are two related rhythms born at approximately the turn of the 20th century.

RHYTHM PATTERNS

It's essential to bear in mind that both of these rhythms share a rhythmic cell of a half bar (all the carioca music is written in 2/4); Brazilians refer to this as *brasileirinho*.

If we repeat this cell, we have the full bar:

For certain variations of the samba and choro, or slow tempo tunes, it is often written as follows:

But since, as you can imagine, marking the two downbeats would not produce enough swing, we must add the syncopation. In the following case, the syncopation is clearly marked, as we will connect the last sixteenth note of each brasileirinho with the first sixteenth note of the following one, resulting in this marvelous pattern:

If the chords were to change, the first sixteenth note of the new chord would be replaced with a rest, and the pattern would look like this:

And if the chord change occurs inside the bar, it would look like this:

Keep in mind that the first chord in each beat may be played in staccato fashion, so you may see this rhythm notated as such:

This is the very heart of Brazilian music! We must take this new pattern and its variations very seriously. If played correctly, they will allow us to enter the marvelous world of Brazilian swing on the guitar.

In samba, the bass notes, which are played by the thumb, will always mark the beats (quarter notes). For this reason, I propose practicing the following example:

Example 1

TRACK 1

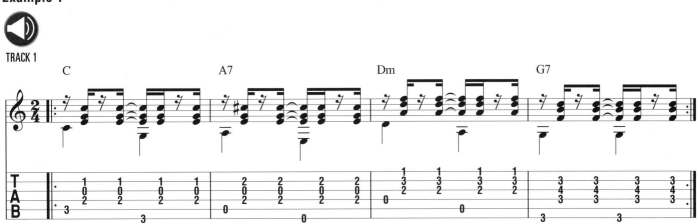

Another way to approach the brasileirinho is by playing the three sixteenth notes after the downbeat. In the previous example, we would thus be left with the following:

Example 2

TRACK 2

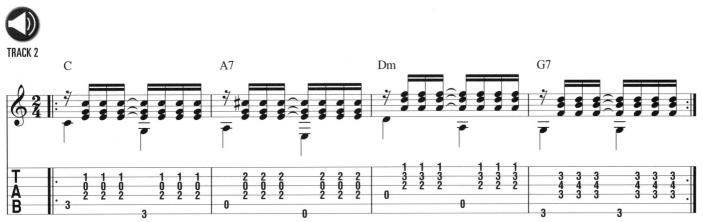

Note that in the examples, the bass is played on the downbeat and alternates between the root and 5th of the chord. This is done to simulate the *surdo*, which is the lowest percussion instrument in the samba percussion ensemble.

Now let's take a look at the song "O Samba da Minha Terra" by Dorival Caymmi. This version is from 1957.

This is the easiest possible way to play samba and is one of the best examples of how the genre was approached before the appearance of bossa nova, which is the moment at which the guitar playing of Brazilian rhythms became more sophisticated.

Let's pay special attention to the following details when playing the song:

- Use of the brasileirinho with three sixteenth notes
- Alternating bass (root-5th) played on the downbeats
- Presence of passing tones (from D to B7)

TRACK 3

O SAMBA DA MINHA TERRA

Sam-ba da mi-nha te-rra dei-xa a gen-te mo-le quan-do se can-ta to-do mun-do bo-

le quan - do se can-ta to-do mun - do bo-le. Sam-ba da mi - nha te-rra dei-xa a gen-te mo-

le quan-do se can-ta to-do mun-do bo-le quan-do se can - ta to-do mun-do bo-

le. Quem não gosta de sam - ba _____ bom su-jei-to não é. _____

Words and Music by Dorival Caymmi
Copyright © 1940 by Editorial Mangione S.A.
Copyright Renewed
All Rights in the United States and Canada Administered by Edward B. Marks Music Company
International Copyright Secured   All Rights Reserved Used by Permission

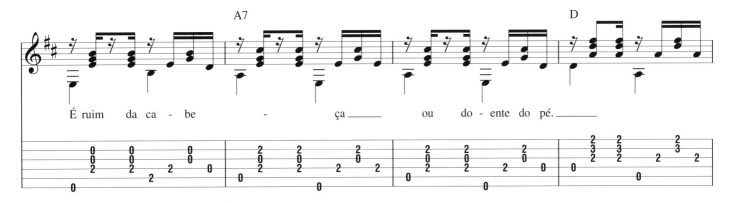

É ruim da ca-be - ça___ ou do-ente do pé.___

Eu nas-ci com o sam - ba___ no sam-ba me cri-ei___

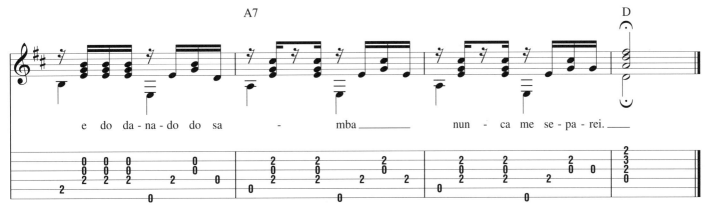

e do da-na-do do sa - mba___ nun - ca me se-pa-rei.___

As you can see, there were times that I played the brasileirinho with the three sixteenth notes broken up, using the index finger of the right hand for the second and fourth sixteenth notes (see bar 8, for example). By playing the higher notes of the chord with my middle and ring fingers on the third sixteenth note, I create a feeling of an accent.

Let's see an example of what we've just done.

Example 3

TRACK 4

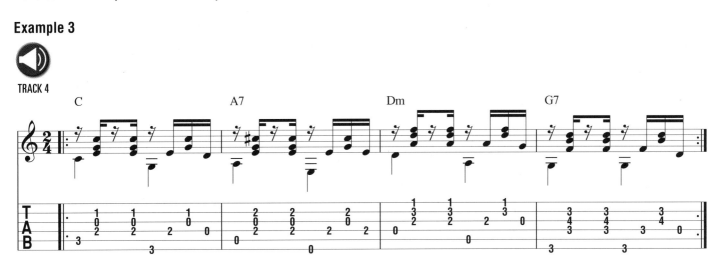

We will soon see that this pattern is going to be essential for playing samba.

SYNCOPATION IN CHORD CHANGES

A big step in terms of making samba swing (in its modern version) can be achieved by syncopating a chord change. Now let's take a look at Example 1, but with syncopation in the chord changes:

Example 4

TRACK 5

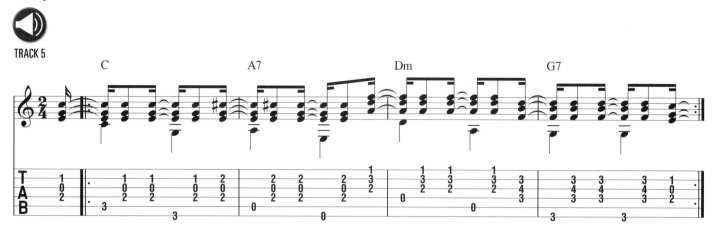

Now we begin to see the most outstanding features that distinguish the choro from the samba:

- The choro generally uses the brasileirinho as shown in Example 1

- The samba generally uses the feel of Example 4 (among others, as we will see further on), syncopating the chord changes

With this in mind, we will begin studying choro.

CHORO

The choro contains many distinguishing elements. Let's take a look at some now.

- Typical instruments:

  a) The guitar provides basic accompaniment and plays the bass notes that provide countermelodies. The seven-string guitar is typical, since it creates more complex melodies with the additional low string, which is generally tuned to C or (in fewer cases) B.

  b) Small string instruments, such as the *cavaquinho* (very similar to the ukulele), mandolin, or banjo provide the rhythm and often take the soloist role.

  c) The *pandeiro* provides percussion rhythmic patterns.

  d) Wind instruments include alto or tenor sax, flute, or clarinet. They generally play solos or counterpoint.

- Harmonies with intensive use of slash chords (with bass notes that differ from the root).

- Modulations: most classic songs modulate to the 4th or 5th (IV or V) scale degrees, to the relative minor, or to the parallel minor mode (generally Aeolian mode).

Now that we have the concepts necessary to understand choro, let's look at our first song, "Carinhoso." This work, composed by Pixinguinha (considered one of the greatest composers within the genre), is from 1917 and is among the top ten choro songs most loved among Brazilians.

CARINHOSO

TRACK 6

Baixarías

For the choro guitar, we must practice in alternating rhythm (the brasileirinho pattern) with counterpoint played in the lower strings of the guitar, which will respond to the lead melody in most cases and fill in the gaps of the verse.

These bass melodic phrases so characteristic of the genre give choro its personality. In Portuguese, they are known as *baixarías*. These are the features of the baixarías:

- They serve as a connection between two chords

- They arpeggiate the chord, usually filling intervals between chord degrees with passing notes

- The melodies tend to move stepwise and chromatically following the same direction (ascending or descending)

- They often use open strings

In "Carinhoso," we see a simple baixaría in the final bars, played on the A7 and Cm6 chords. In that case, the baixaría prepares the E♭7.

Let's look at some other baixarías examples.

Example 1

TRACK 7

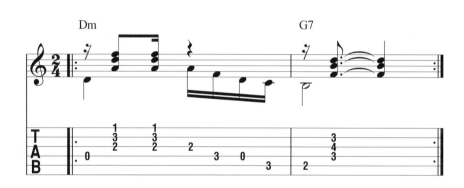

Example 2

TRACK 8

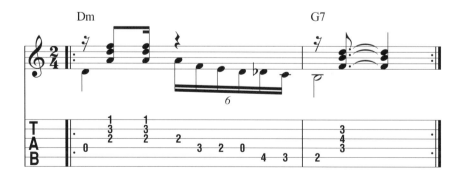

Example 3

TRACK 9

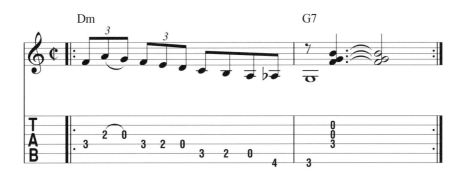

Example 4

TRACK 10

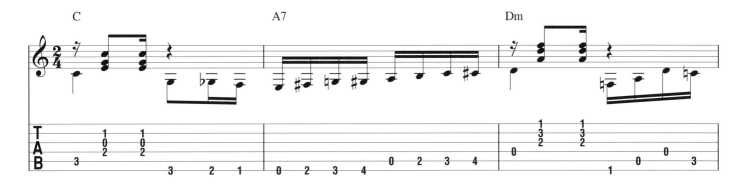

In the following song, "As Rosas Não Falam," we will see that the baixarías are quite more complex. The guitar player who recorded this song on Cartola's emblematic *Cartola* (I and II) records is Dino 7 Cordas ("Seven-String Dino"), a pioneer and point of reference in the seven-string playing style. The concepts and musical phrases he developed were used by all choro guitar players, and his influence in the style is universal.

It's important to note that Dino alternates between binary and ternary subdivisions (eighth- and sixteenth-note triplets), as seen in the previous examples, and this is what makes his lines so unique.

AS ROSAS NÃO FALAM

TRACK 11

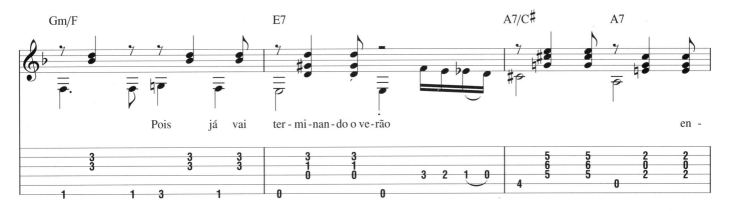

BAIXARÍAS CONCEPTS

In order to master the "baixarías" style, one must have a solid understanding of the following concepts:

Melodic Concepts

Scales:

- Major

- Minor (with it variations melodic minor and harmonic minor)

- Chromatic scale

- Diminished and augmented scales

Arpeggios:

- Triads (major, minor, diminished, and augmented)

- Four-voice chords (maj7, m7, 7, m7♭5, m[maj7], °7, and +7)

- Chords with extensions and alterations (all of the previous chords with additional scale tones or altered tensions)

Rhythmic Concepts

- Rhythm cells using binary subdivision

- Rhythm cells using ternary subdivision

- Combination of binary and ternary subdivisions

Now we will see another choro example on a faster tempo. In this song, "Noites Cariocas," we can again appreciate the great baixarías played by Dino 7 Cordas.

TRACK 12

NOITES CARIOCAS

24

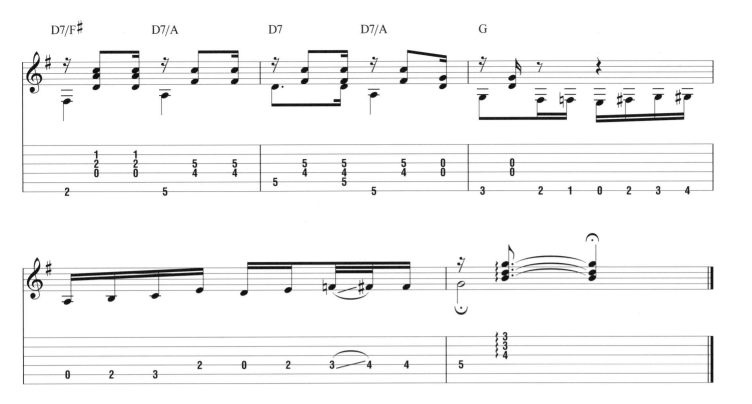

SAMBA

Samba is the carioca rhythm par excellence, and thus the rhythm of Brazil. Although its younger sibling, the bossa nova, is more well-known throughout the world, the samba is the rhythm that best represents the essence of Brazilian music and culture.

As we saw earlier, the basic rhythmic cell is the brasileirinho, but it is important to note the syncopation in both a single chord or in chord changes.

The first sambas share many of the choro's features, including the baixarías, but since it was a more popular style at the beginning, it did not require the technical expertise that characterizes choro guitar. Samba musicians generally played this rhythm in a much simpler way.

The samba's basic pattern, along with the brasileirinho, is the following:

In the next song, a samba classic called "Filosofia do Samba," we can see how samba interacts with its older sibling the choro. Since both styles are closely related in historical, geographical, and cultural terms, they have many mutual influences. The features that I emphasize (which we have already seen) are the following:

- Syncopation in chord changes
- Typical samba pattern
- Use of the baixarías (so typical of choro, now applied in samba)

FILOSOFIA DO SAMBA

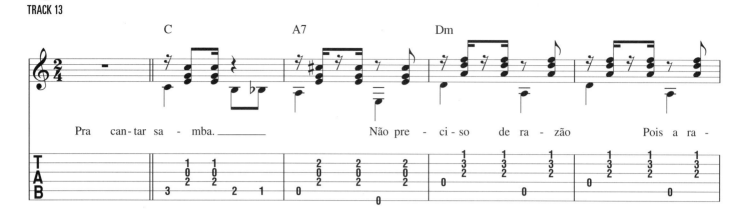

Pra can-tar sa - mba._____ Não pre - ci-so de ra - zão Pois a ra-

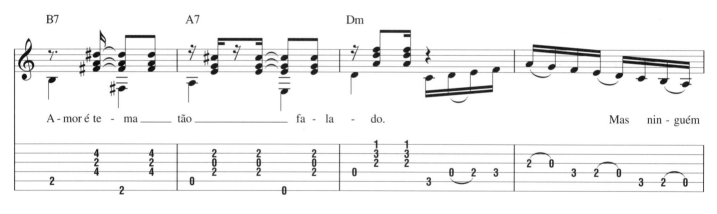

zão._____ Es - tá sem - pre com os dois la - dos.

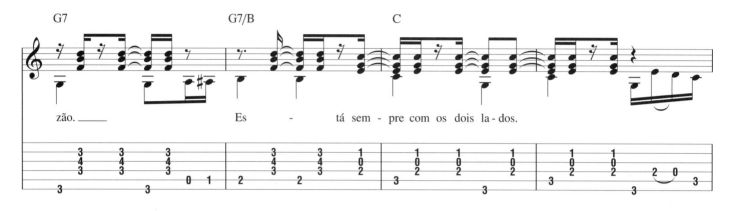

A - mor é te - ma _____ tão _____ fa - la - do. Mas nin - guém

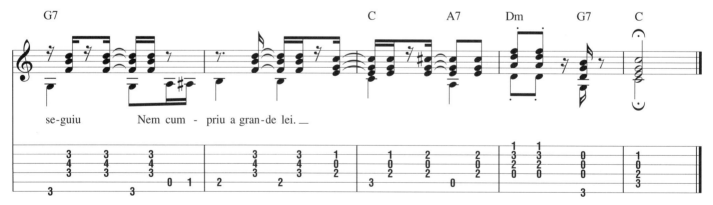

se-guiu Nem cum - priu a gran-de lei.__

Words and Music by Antonio Candeia
© 1971 (Renewed 1999) EDICOES MUSICAIS TAPAJOS LTDA.
All Rights Controlled and Administered by EMI APRIL MUSIC INC.

Let's see how the samba pattern would look if we change its first cell for a brasileirinho.

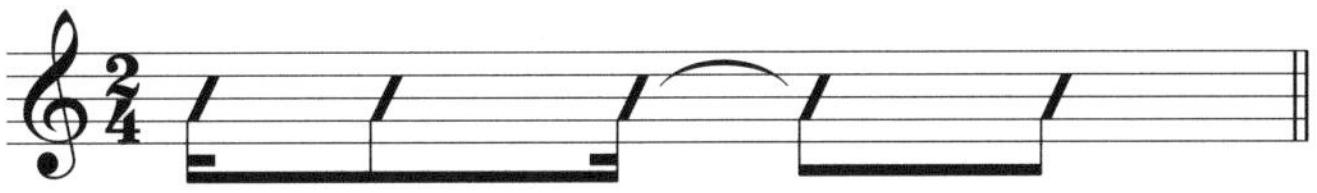

We'll now apply a concept often used in African rhythms, which is to switch the cells of a pattern. So the pattern that we've just seen would look like this:

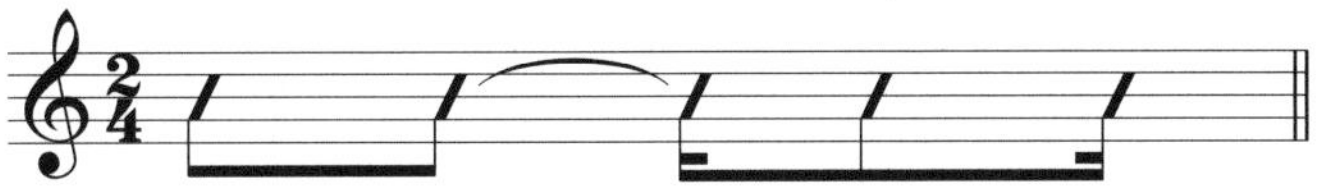

And if now we combine the samba pattern (with the brasileirinho) and this last pattern, we would get the following:

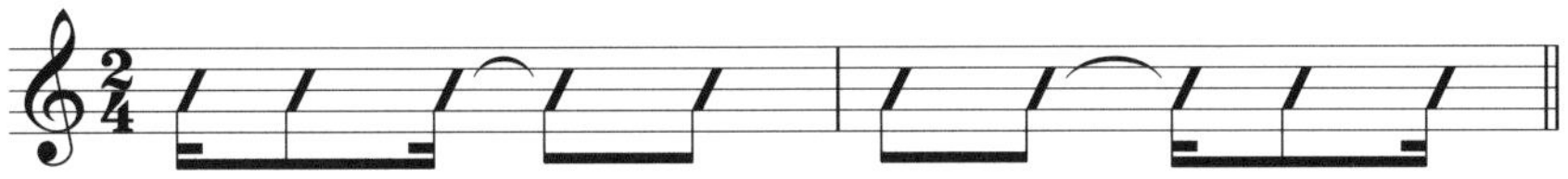

And what would make sense now, since this is a samba pattern? Right! Add syncopation, which gives us:

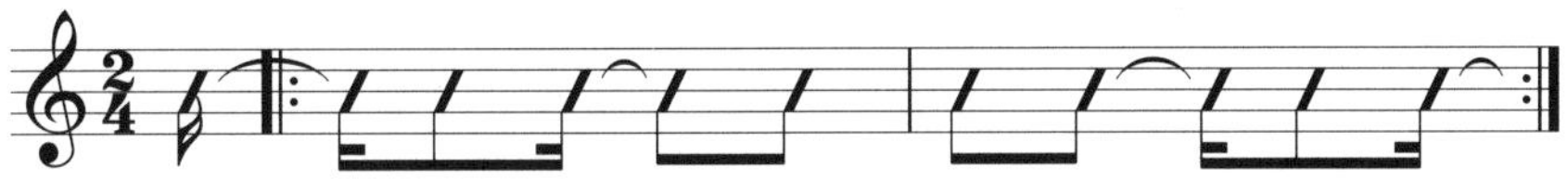

This is the typical samba pattern. Here's an example:

Example 1

TRACK 14

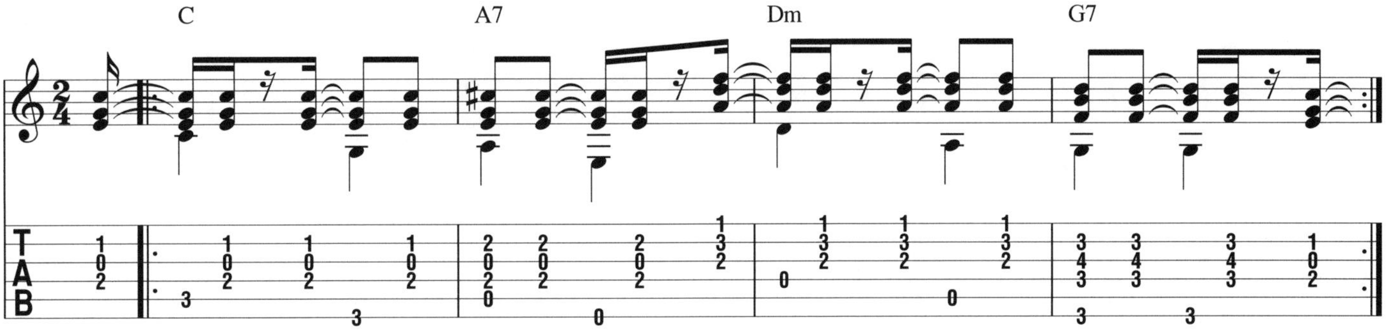

The next song, "Aquarela Brasileira," is the most well-known samba of all time. It was composed by Ary Barroso, one of the most renowned composers of Brazilian music. Some of the other interesting techniques that we find in this particular samba tune are the following:

- Line clichés on major and minor chords—there are chromatic movements of an internal chord voice (as we saw in the first chords of "Carinhoso")
- Chromatic seventh chord movements
- Bass line with the addition of a sixteenth note (emulating a bass player's samba groove)

AQUARELA BRASILEIRA
(AQUARELA DO BRASIL)

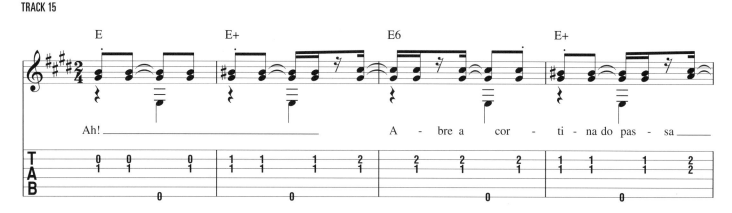

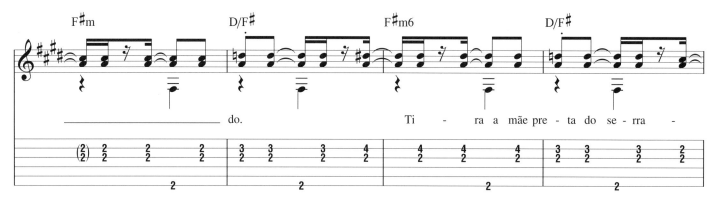

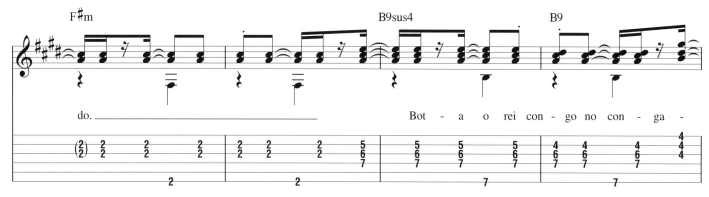

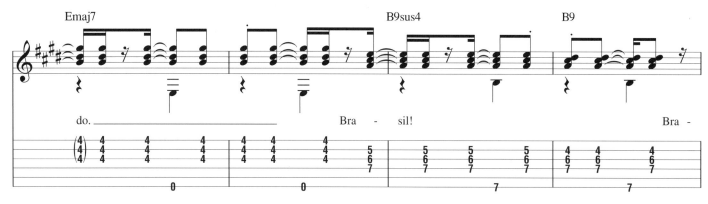

Words and Music by Ary Barroso
Copyright © 1939 by Irmaos Vitale
Copyright Renewed
All Rights for the World excluding Brazil Administered by Peer International Corporation

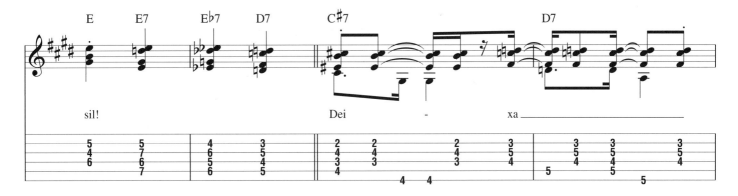

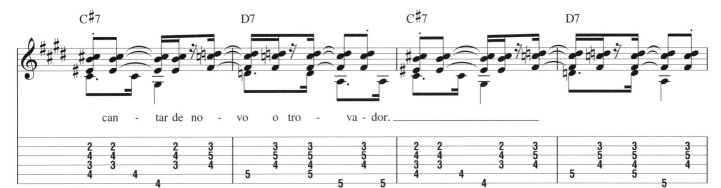

ver   a   Sá Do - na ca - mi - nhan -   do. _____

Pe -   los sa - lões arras - ta -   do. _____

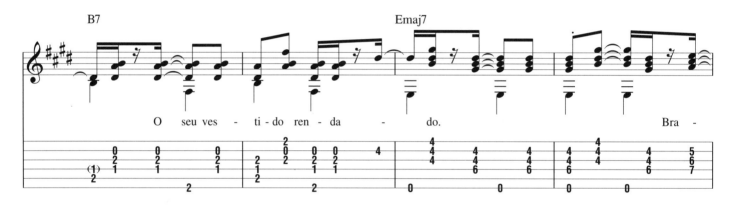

O   seu ves - ti - do ren - da -   do.   Bra -

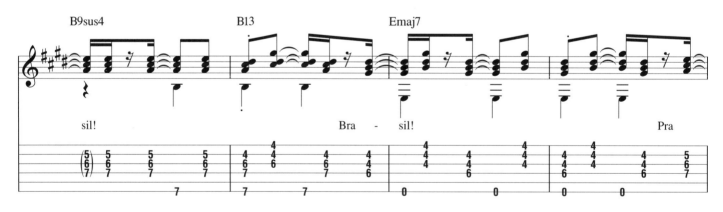

sil!   Bra - sil!   Pra

mim   pra   mim.

Samba Variations

Several sub-genres have arisen from samba. The two that I will present in this book are *samba partido alto* and *samba rock*.

In its guitar adaptation, partido alto is a rhythmic variation on samba that is defined by a particular way of playing its typical pattern. Its main feature is the marked accent on the second sixteenth note of the samba pattern.

We'll use the following patterns:

In this variation, the second beat of the first measure is syncopated.

As we saw in previous sambas (when we noted the use of the left hand index), the contrast that is made when we change the set of strings played creates an accent. This feeling is critical to creating the unique flavor of the partido alto execution. In partido alto, the same effect is achieved by alternating between the string sets 4–3–2 and 3–2–1. With that approach, the pattern looks like this:

Let's look at an example of this idea:

Example 1

TRACK 16

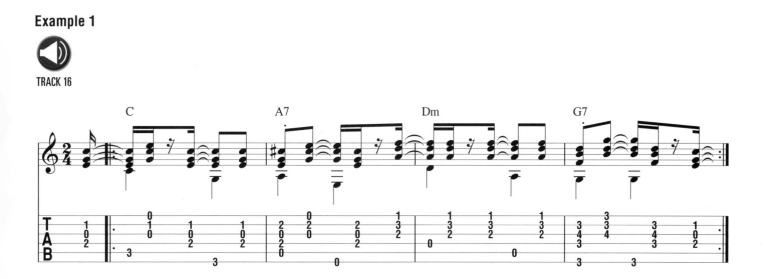

As we can see in this example, I also emphasize the second eighth note of the second bar using the same change of the string set, thus obtaining the same accent effect.

The partido alto song I've chosen is "Linha de Passe," by João Bosco. Bosco's technique is impeccable on both the vocal and the guitar, and he's one of the most outstanding exponents of this musical genre.

LINHA DE PASSE

TRACK 17

To - ca de ta - tu, lin - güi - ça e pa - io e boi ze - bu. Ra -

ba - da com an - gu, ra - bo de sa - ia.

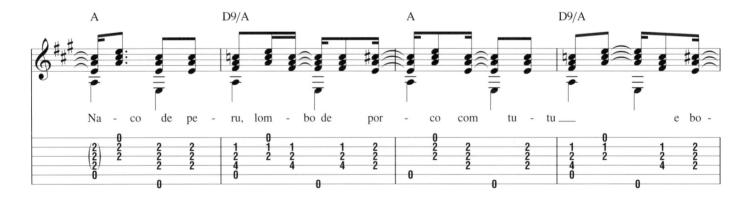

Na - co de pe - ru, lom - bo de por - co com tu - tu ___ e bo -

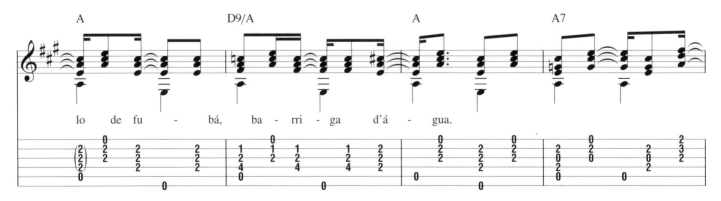

lo de fu - bá, ba - rri - ga d'á - gua.

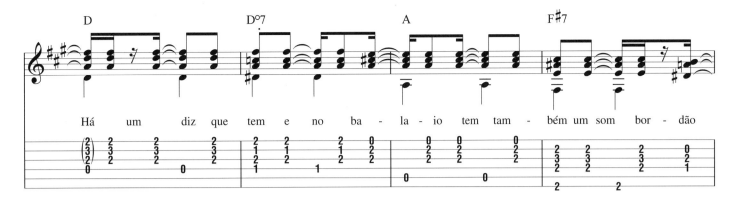

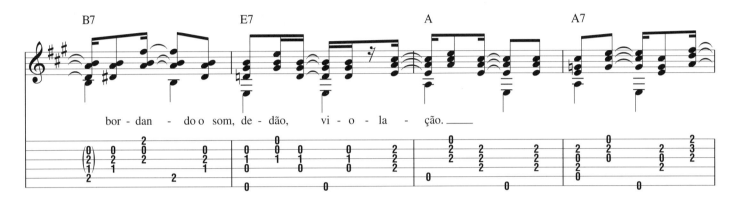

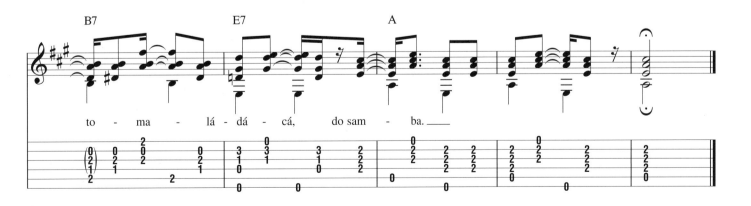

Another samba subgenre is samba rock, which was popularized by Jorge Benjor, a composer of Brazilian popular music classics like "Mais que Nada," "Pais Tropical," and others.

The fundamental features of samba rock are the following:

- Played with a guitar pick
- Samba patterns with extensive use of left-hand muting (similar to funk, which is why it is often referred to as "samba funk").

Let's see an example.

Note that this is closely related to the characteristic samba pattern, but we're starting on the downbeat in this case. Let's see a variation:

And here's the song "Por Causa de Vocé Menina" by Jorge Benjor.

POR CAUSA DE VOCÉ MENINA

TRACK 18

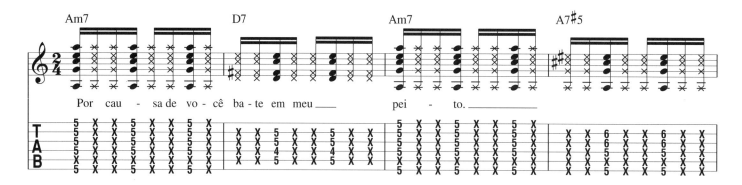

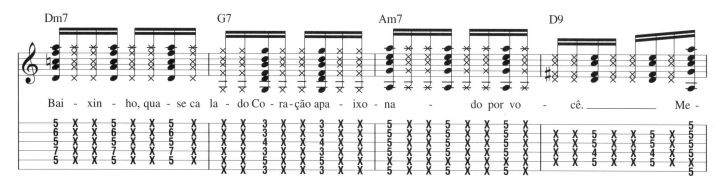

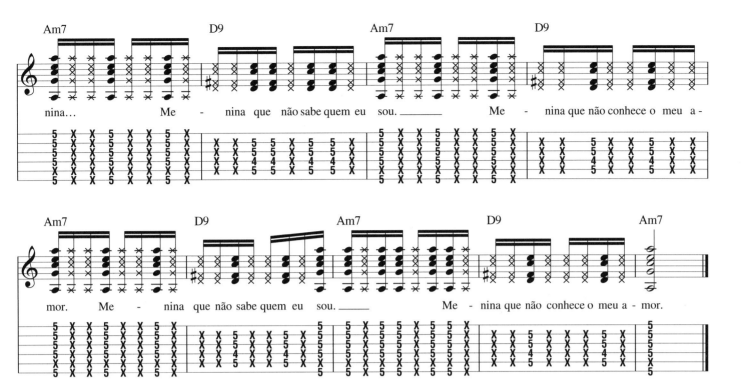

nina... Me - nina que não sabe quem eu sou._____ Me - nina que não conhece o meu a-

mor. Me - nina que não sabe quem eu sou._____ Me - nina que não conhece o meu a - mor.

BOSSA NOVA

Bossa nova is the rhythm for which Brazil is most well-known worldwide. It has many different influences, but the strongest are unquestionably samba and jazz. To put it simply, bossa nova combines the rhythm of samba with the harmony of jazz. The main features of this style are as follows:

- Slow to moderate tempos

- Rhythmic patterns of samba adapted to these tempos

- Rhythm section ensembles

- Use of four-voice harmonies, emphasizing *voice leading* with stepwise and chromatic movements of internal chord voices

Voice Leading

Voice leading is a technique for analyzing how the different "voices" (the different notes or intervals that make up each chord) move between one chord and the next. Let's look at the following chord progression:

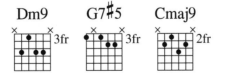

As you can see, as we move from one chord to the next, the top voice (note) in the chord descends by half steps.

Just as we analyze the movement of the top voice (also called the *soprano*), we can do the same with the middle voices as well as with the bass. In bossa nova, the idea is to use the shortest possible movements between one chord and the next, ideally moving just a half step at a time. Now we will look at several examples of voice leading. I will use guitar grids to graphically demonstrate the movement of the voices from one chord to the next.

One Chord Examples

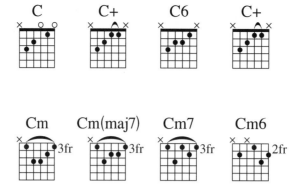

Major ii-V-I (using tritone substitution)

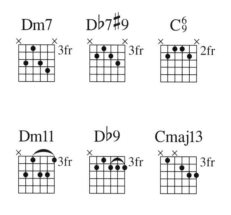

Minor ii-V-i

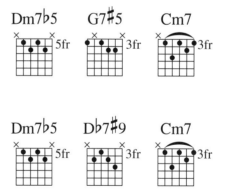

João Gilberto was responsible for developing bossa nova on guitar. What distinguished Gilberto was the way he simplified the samba rhythms on his right hand while playing four-voice chords (using many extensions and alterations) with a considerable focus on voice leading.

João works on different bossa nova patterns. In my book *Bossa Nova Guitar* (Hal Leonard), I have described all of these patterns and their variations step by step. Let's see the two main ones here:

Pattern 1

Pattern 2

This example demonstrates how they sound when combined.

Example 1

TRACK 19

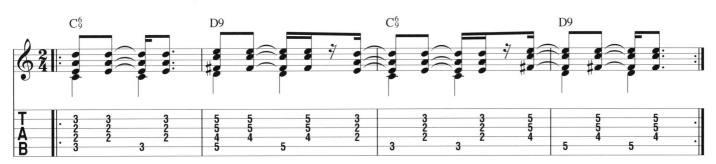

Now I'll add a variation to this pattern using a concept that we've already seen in samba, which is to invert the cells of a pattern. Let's do this with Pattern 2, which features syncopation on the sixteenth note.

This pattern is generally preceded by Pattern 2. Let's take a look at the previous example, now adding this new pattern on its last bar:

Example 2

TRACK 20

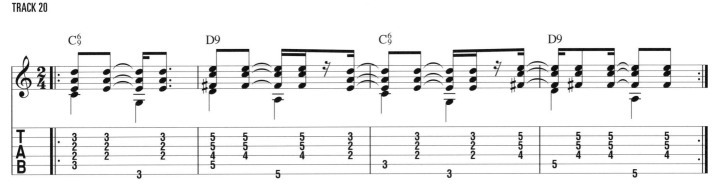

This first bossa nova song was recorded by João Gilberto on the Elizeth Cardozo record *Canção de Amor Demais* and is called "Chega de Saudade." This song is an icon of the bossa nova style.

CHEGA DE SAUDADE

TRACK 21

Original Text by Vinicius de Moraes
Music by Antonio Carlos Jobim

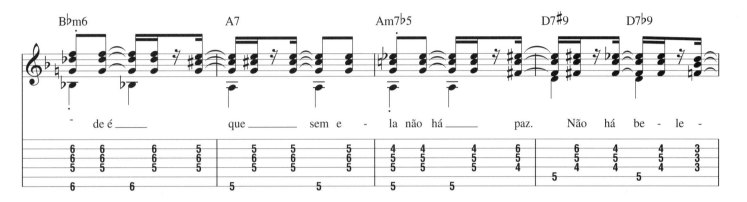

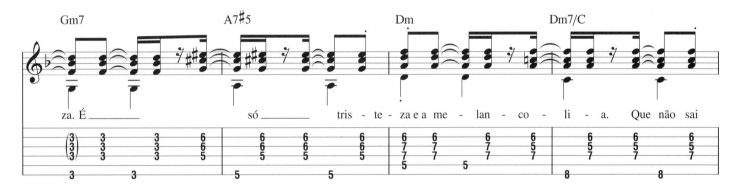

As can be seen in bars 16, 24, and 30, I used the brasileirinho. Because of its close connection to bossa and samba, you will see that it is used quite frequently.

Another pattern that is frequently used is the one we saw earlier: the "Typical Samba Pattern." In bossa nova, this is played in a more relaxed, delicate way, which gives the style its own personality (along with the four-note chords, as we already saw). João Gilberto used this pattern many times as the base for an entire song, so we should note its important role in bossa nova.

Pattern 3

In the following bossa nova classic, "O Barquinho" (or "Little Boat") by Roberto Menescal, we'll see how this new pattern is used.

O BARQUINHO

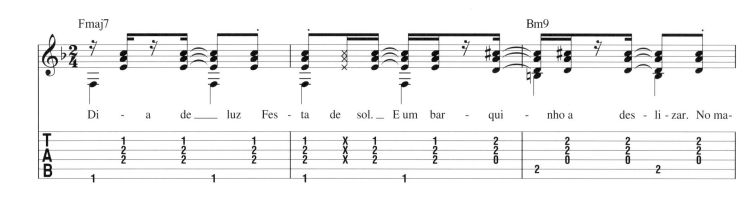

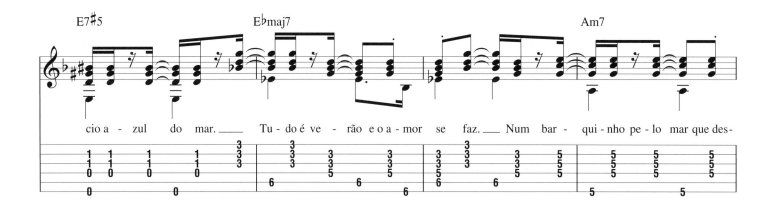

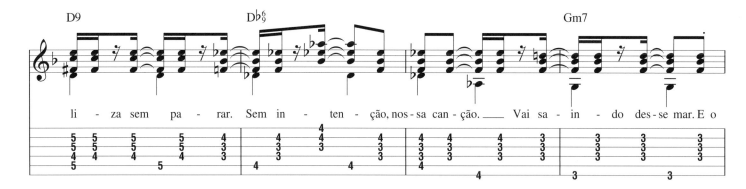

Original Lyric by Ronaldo Boscoli
English Lyric by Buddy Kaye
Music by Roberto Menescal
Copyright © 1963 EDITIONS SACHA S.A.R.L.
Copyright Renewed
All Rights for the U.S. and Canada Controlled and Administered by SONGS OF UNIVERSAL, INC.
All Rights Reserved   Used by Permission

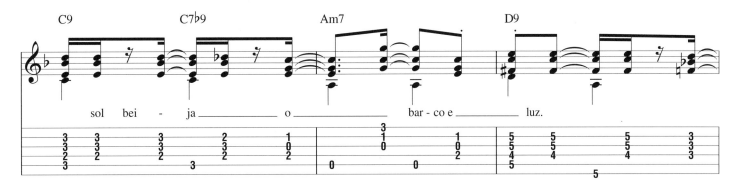

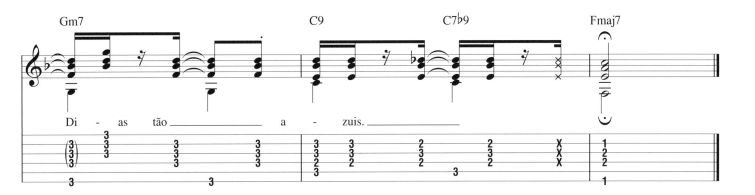

More Complex Bossa Nova Patterns

On guitar, bossa nova offers a universe of possibilities in terms of harmony, rhythm, and guitar technique. The most important are the following:

Chords

- Intensive use of extensions (9ths, 11ths, and 13ths)

- Sus and add chords (like 7sus9, 7sus9/11, minor add9, etc.)

- Chord inversions (chords in which a tone other than the root is in the bass)

Rhythm

- Complex, combined 16th-note rhythm cells

- Intensive use of anticipation and syncopation

Guitar Technique

- Muting by the left hand

- Independence of the index finger

- Right-hand dynamics

The following song, "Desafinado," is highly sophisticated in terms of harmony, melody, and rhythm. We'll use it to demonstrate the most comprehensive way of playing bossa nova, in which all of the techniques that we've seen come into play.

DESAFINADO

TRACK 23

Original Text by Newton Mendonça
Music by Antonio Carlos Jobim
Copyright © 1959, 1962 Editora Musical Arapua
All Rights for the U.S. Administered by Corcovado Music Corp. and Bendig Music Corp.
All Rights for Canada Administered by Bendig Music Corp.
International Copyright Secured   All Rights Reserved

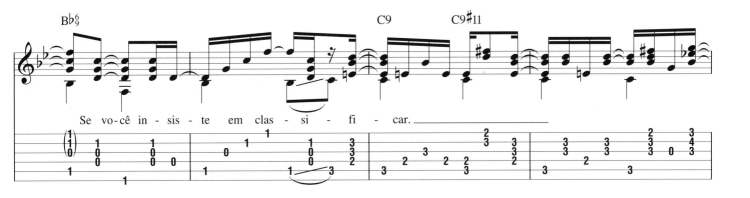

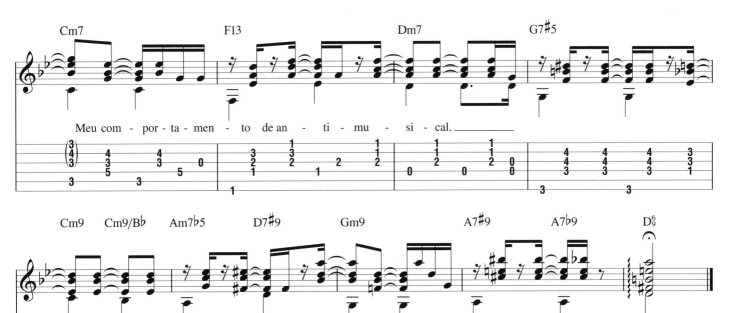

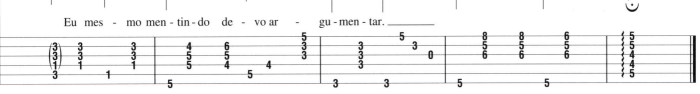

Chord Melody

To provide an example of a bossa nova chord melody, I have transcribed "Samba do Avião," a beautiful composition by Tom Jobim honoring his city, Rio de Janeiro. This version, transcribed note-for-note, was played by the most talented guitar player in the history of Brazil: Baden Powell.

In this version, we'll discover all of the rhythmic elements that make up bossa nova, elements of samba and choro (baixarías), and, as if that weren't enough, a majestic chord melody to boot.

Chord melody playing in bossa nova is very unique. It's important to be constantly emphasizing the rhythmic patterns and combining them with the song melody. So we'll be playing rhythm guitar most of the time along with the chord changes and the lead melody.

To start, let's analyze some other features that appear on this transcription:

- **Use of syncopated bass:** as with all of the previous examples of samba and bossa nova, in which the internal chord voices (played with the IMR block) are syncopated, we will see the presence of syncopated bass notes. When this happens, the IMR block is usually played on the downbeat.

- **Use of quartal harmony:** chords whose tones are separated by perfect 4th intervals.

SAMBA DO AVIÃO

Words and Music by Antonio Carlos Jobim

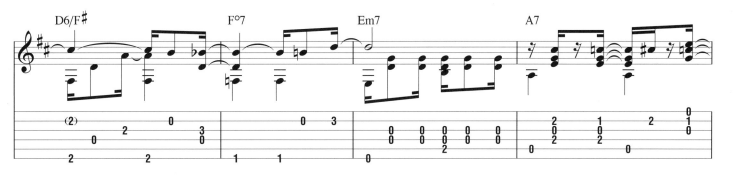

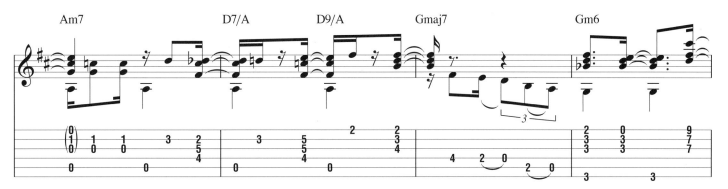

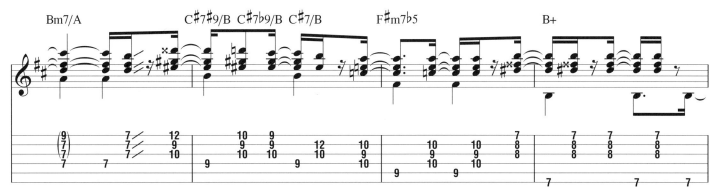

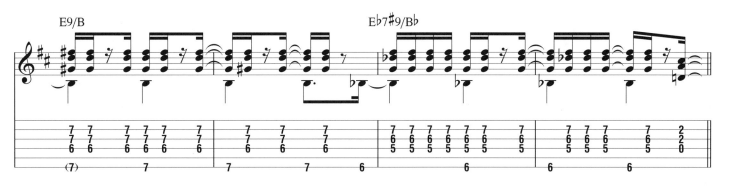

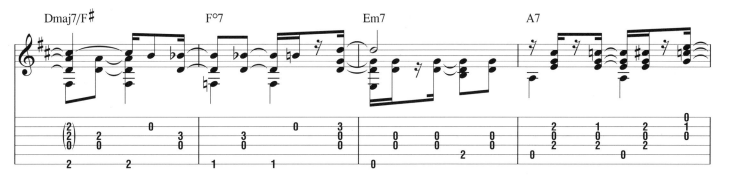

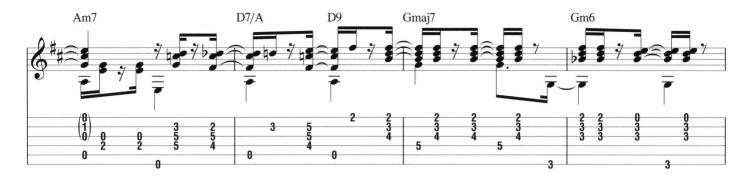

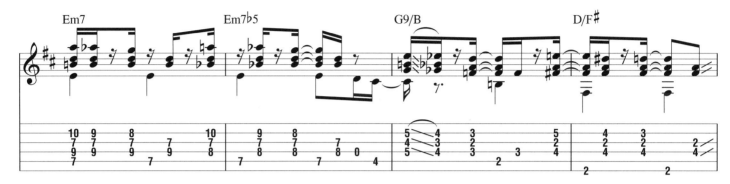

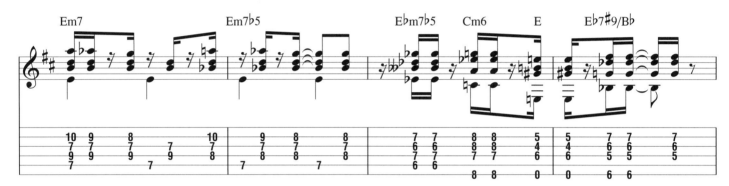

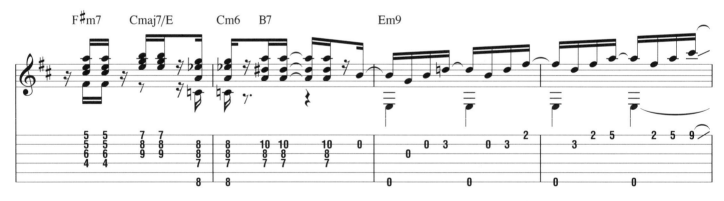

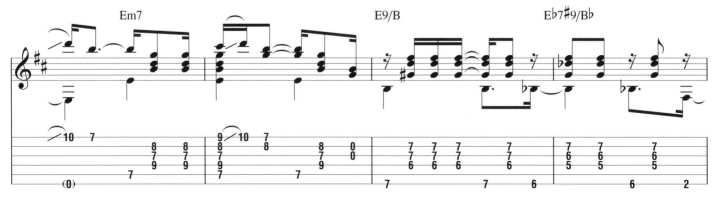

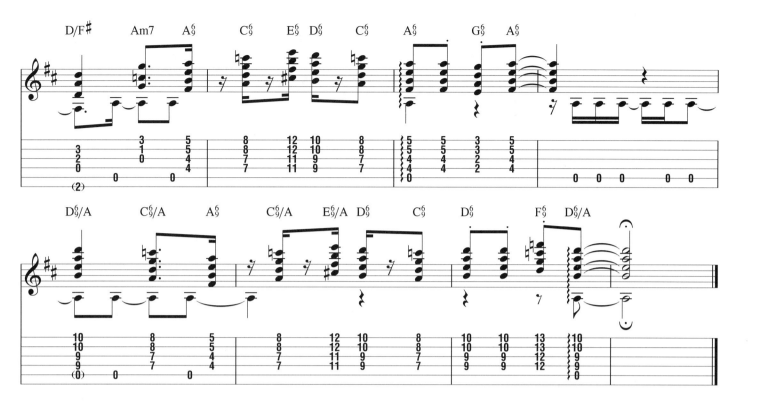

CHAPTER 3: RHYTHMS FROM NORTHEAST BRAZIL

Northeast Brazil has a long list of rhythms of its own. Its most well-known genres include *baião*, *xote*, *frevo*, *afoxé*, and *marcha rancho*. We'll analyze each of the rhythms as we've done with the others.

BAIÃO

This rhythm was developed by Luiz Gonzaga, a composer and *sanfona* player (the *sanfona* is similar to the accordion). Its typical instrumentation and their functions are as such:

- Sanfona: harmony

- *Zabumba*: bass percussive sounds

- Triangle: subdivision, sixteenth-note patterns

The main rhythmic feature of baião is that the bass notes follow this pattern:

The variations are created by replacing some of the figures of the patterns with rests. Here are a few examples.

A frequent variation on these last two patterns is created by replacing the *i-m-r* block in the first eighth note of the second beat with the index finger. In the following example, you will notice the difference as I play the first bar with the *i-m-r* block and the second with the index finger.

Example 1

TRACK 25

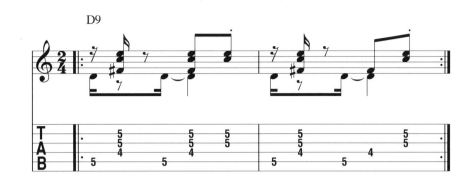

Example 2

TRACK 26

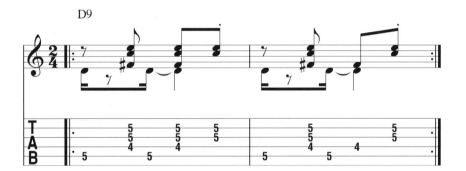

BAIÃO RHYTHM

Two important facts to consider for mastering baião rhythm:

- The bass syncopates the second pulse.

- The harmonies and melodies are usually from the Mixolydian and Lydian ♭7 modes.

Now let's take a look at the song "Asa Branca," which is an emblematic baião tune composed by Luiz Gonzaga, who's known in Brazil as "the king of baião."

ASA BRANCA

TRACK 27

XOTE

The gatherings where people dance the folk rhythms of the northeast are called *forrós*. At these dances, most of the rhythms are baião and xote.

The instrumentation of xote is the same as baião, but the rhythmic marking and the bass notes are slightly different. Its classic rhythmic patterns are the following:

It is important to work the bass notes, because marking its typical lines on the bass strings of the guitar is a fundamental aspect of this genre.

The next song, "O Xote das Meninas" by Luiz Gonzaga, is also a classic.

O XOTE DAS MENINAS

Words and Music by Luiz Gonzaga and Ze Dantas
Copyright © 1953 by Irmaos Vitale Comercio E Industria
Copyright Renewed
All Rights Controlled and Administered by Peer International Corporation
International Copyright Secured   All Rights Reserved

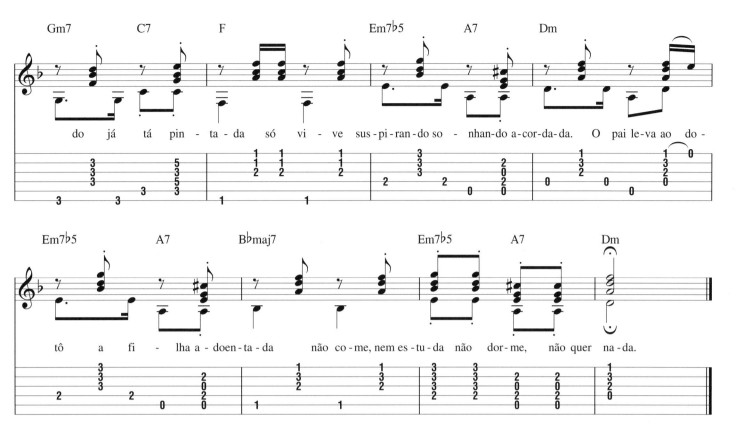

do já tá pin-ta-da só vi-ve sus-pi-ran-do so — nhan-do a-cor-da-da. O pai le-va ao do-

tô a fi — lha a-doen-ta-da não co-me, nem es-tu-da não dor-me, não quer na-da.

AFOXÉ

This style comes from Salvador Bahía and is based upon Afro-Brazilian religious rituals. It's spread far beyond its origins in the carnivals of Bahía and Pernambuco and is now interpreted by such artists as Caetano Veloso and Gilberto Gil.

Its main feature is the use of the syncopated bass notes, but unlike what we have seen up until now, the syncopated note is the eighth note. The basic pattern is the following:

Example 1

TRACK 29

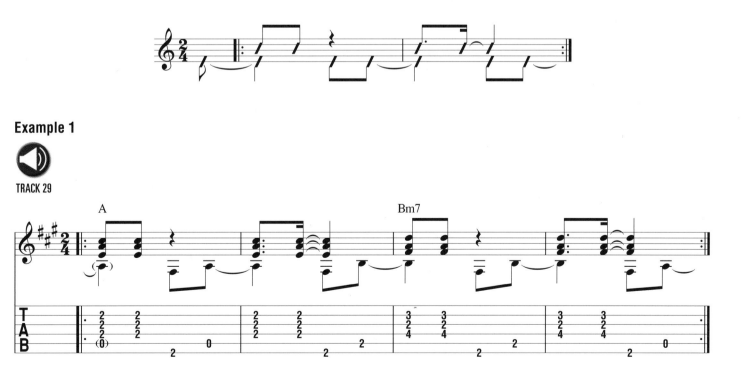

Let's look at a common variation:

Example 2

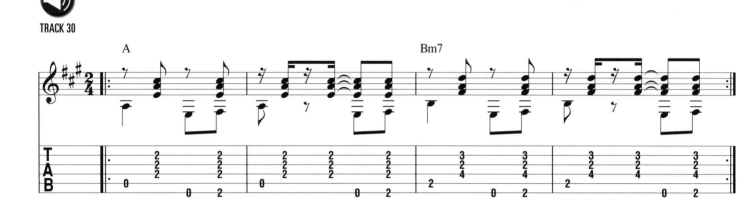

In the following song, "Toda Menina Baiana," composer and musician Gilberto Gil presents us with the ideal way for getting to know this musical style. Pay special attention to the bass lines that Gil plays. They anticipate the root (or the bass if it's a slash chord) in a way characteristic of this genre.

TODA MENINA BAIANA

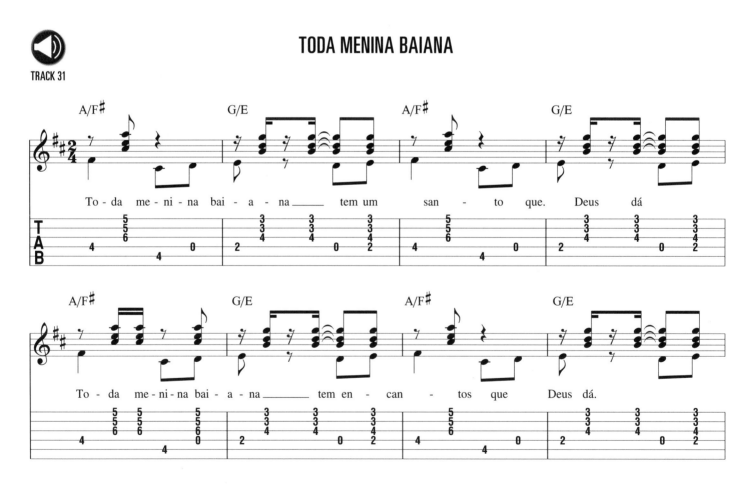

Words and Music by Gilberto Gil
© 1979 Preta Music
All Rights Reserved   Used by Permission

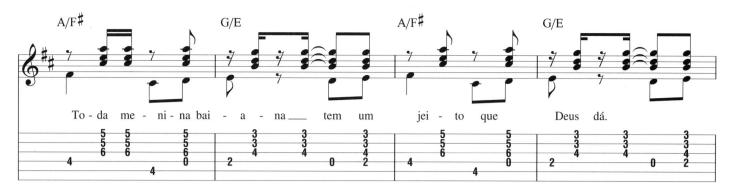

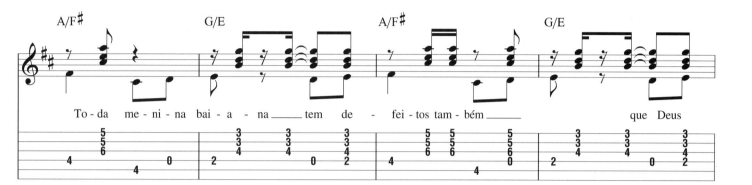

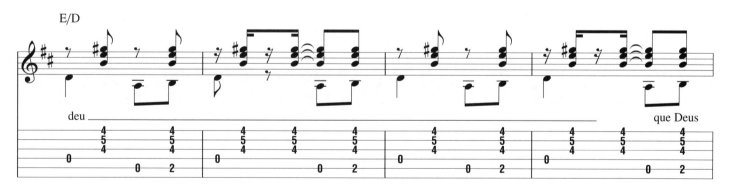

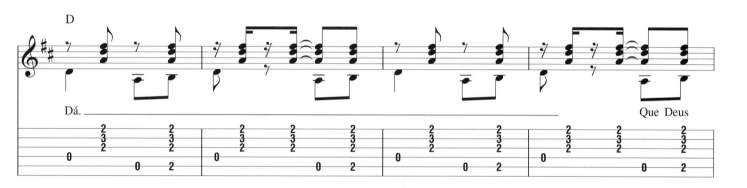

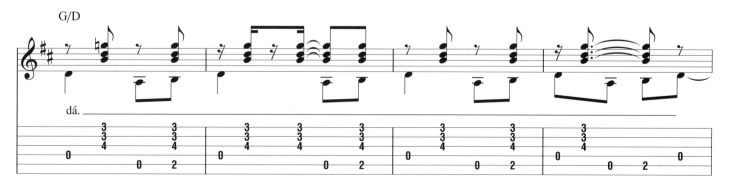

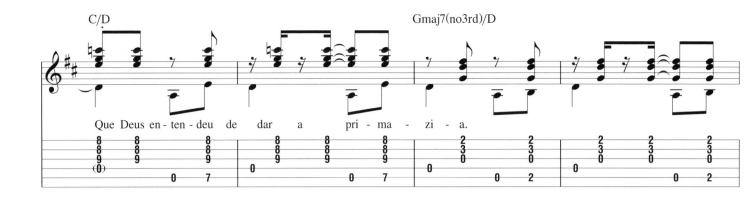

Que Deus en - ten - deu de dar a pri - ma - zi - a.

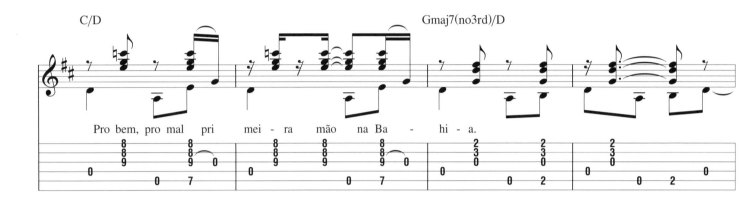

Pro bem, pro mal pri mei - ra mão na Ba - hi - a.

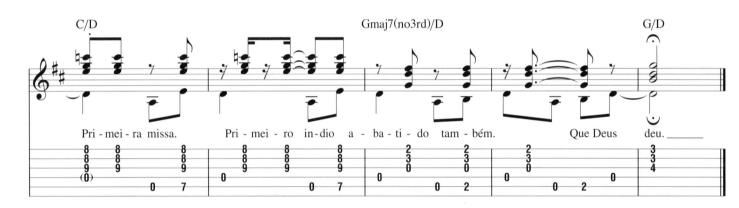

Pri - mei - ra missa. Pri - mei - ro in - dio a - ba - ti - do tam - bém. Que Deus deu. _____

AFOXÉ ORIGINS

Afoxé is a variation of *Ixejá*, the rhythmic style commonly used in *Candomblé* ceremonies, the Afro-Brazilian religion that is popular in the Bahía region in Northeastern Brazil. As with most of the Latin American rhythms of African descent, the guitar emulates various percussion instruments. In the case of the Afoxé, that includes the:

- Atabaque (in its three variations: *rum, pi*, and *lê*)

- Agogô

- Xequerê

FREVO

This rhythm, which hails from the city of Pernambuco, was first played by military bands. It's very popular in the carnival celebrations of this city in northeast Brazil. The main characteristics of frevo are:

- Fast tempos (120 bpm or greater)
- Emphasized bass notes, often alternating between the root and the 5th of the chord

The most commonly used guitar patterns are the following:

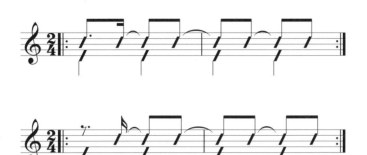

The song we'll see here is "Festa do Interior," which was composed by Moraes Moreira and made world-famous by singer Gal Costa. I've transcribed her version of the song below.

TRACK 32

FESTA DO INTERIOR

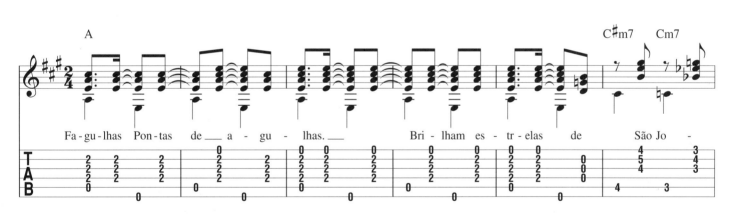

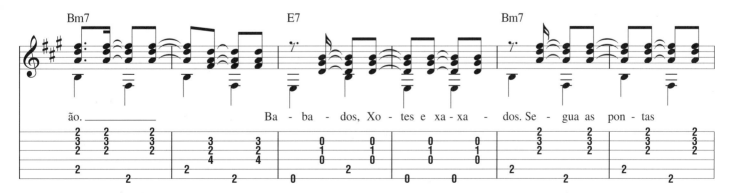

By Moraes Moreira and Abel Silva
© 1981 WARNER/CHAPPELL EDICOES MUSICAIS LTDA. and EDICOES MUSICAIS TAPAJOS LTDA.
All Rights for WARNER/CHAPPELL EDICOES MUSICAIS LTDA. Administered by WB MUSIC CORP.
All Rights for EDICOES MUSICAIS TAPAJOS LTDA. Controlled and Administered by EMI BLACKWOOD MUSIC INC.
All Rights Reserved   Used by Permission

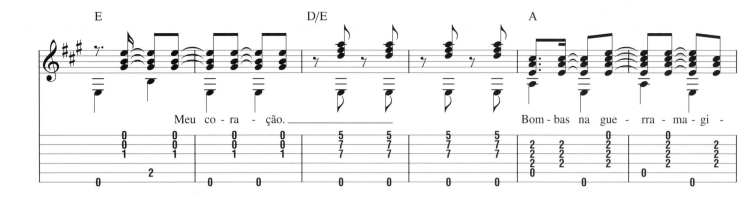

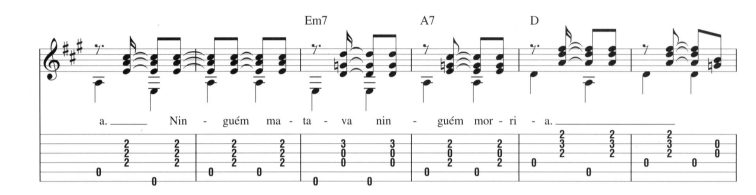

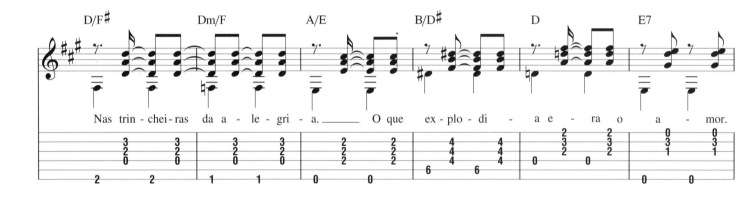

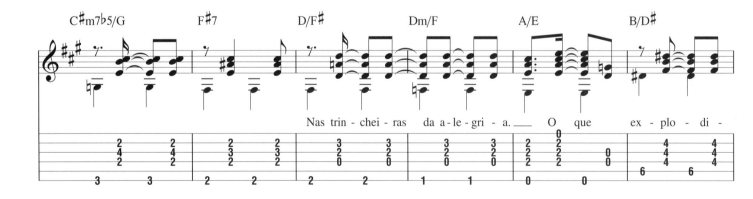

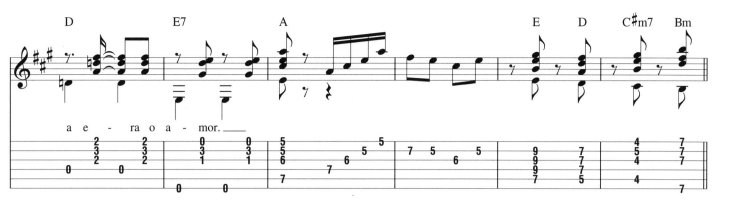

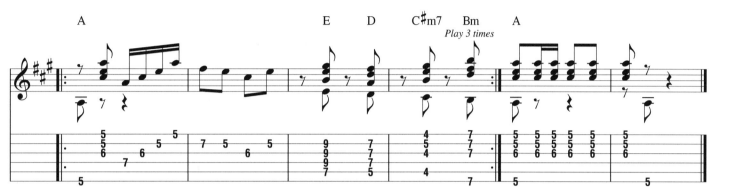

MARCHA RANCHO

Marcha rancho is a derivative of frevo. Both share the same basic features, but marcha rancho is played in a more relaxed way. The pattern we're going to use is the following:

To demonstrate this rhythm, we'll look at the song "Entrudo" by Carlos Lyra, a famous composer from the 1960s.

ENTRUDO

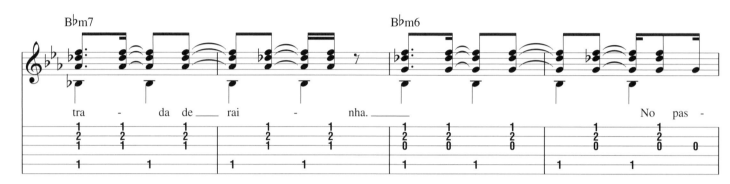

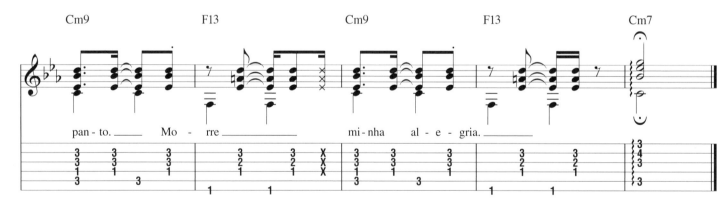

Words and Music by Ruy Guerra and Carlos Lyra
Copyright © 1972 Guanabara Music c/o Scion Three Music LLC and Ruy Guerra Publishing
Copyright Renewed
International Copyright Secured   All Rights Reserved

GLOSSARY

afoxé: Brazilian ritual *candomblé* music from the northeastern coastal state of Bahia. Parading carnival groups (blocos afro), especially around the city of Salvadore, have adopted the music for decades. Tradition began with Bloco Pandegos da Africa (Revelers of Africa) in the 1890s, thrived, and then by the early 1970s, the only group left was Filhos de Ghandhy.

baião: Often confused with *forró* (some say a division of *forró* , others that *forró* is a very fast baião), this was a 19th century folkloric circle dance from the northeast of Brazil. Original instrumentation was the guitar (later accordion or *sanfona*), triangle, and *zabumba* bass drum. In the mid to late 1940s, the baião and the *forró* were transformed and popularized by Luiz Gonzaga.

baixarías: Contrapuntal melodic bass line usually played by a 7-string guitar (nylon-string guitar with an added bass string tuned to C, or sometimes B). It is a main characteristic of the *choro* genre. Baixaría is a second melodic line that is akin to the bass part of a two-part invention by Bach.

bossa nova: Musical style originated in Rio de Janeiro that evolved from *samba* but is more harmonically complex and less percussive. As opposed to *samba's* origins in the favelas (Brazilian shanty towns), bossa nova emerged primarily from the upscale beachside neighborhoods of Rio de Janeiro. Certain similar elements were already evident, even influences from classical music like Debussy and Ravel, and jazz styles such as cool jazz. The style was developed by Tom Jobim, João Gilberto, and Vinicius de Moraes.

brasileirinho: A rhythmic cell composed of one sixteenth note followed by an eighth note and another sixteenth note. This cell is the basis of *samba* rhythm.

candomblé: An Afro-Brazilian religion primarily practiced in Bahia that is most closely related to old West African practices. Candomblé is often referred to as "macumba" in Rio de Janeiro and São Paulo.

carioca: A person born or living in Rio de Janeiro.

cavaquinho: Small string instrument of the European guitar family with four wire or gut strings. It is a very important instrument in Brazilian music, especially for *samba* and *choro*.

choro: A Brazilian genre of popular instrumental music that originated in 19th century Rio de Janeiro. It means "cry" or "lament," but despite its name, the music often has a fast and happy rhythm. It is characterized by virtuosity, improvisation, and subtle modulations, and is full of syncopation and counterpoint. Choro is considered the first characteristically Brazilian genre of urban popular music. Typical instrumentation includes a *cavaquinho*, two nylon-string guitars (including a 7-string guitar), a *pandeiro*, and two instruments for soloing, which are typically a flute and a saxophone.

choro-samba: A *choro* hybrid that is sung with melodramatic lyrics dealing with love and unhappiness.

forrós: A popular genre of music and dance in Brazil's Northeast, to the extent that historically "going to the forró" meant simply going to party or going out. Regarding the music, it is based on a combination of three instruments (*sanfona, zabumba*, and a metal triangle). The dance, however, becomes very different as you cross the borders of the Northeast into the Southeast.

frevo: A wide range of musical styles originating from Recife, state of Pernambuco. The word "frevo" is said to come from "frever," a misspeaking of the Portuguese word *ferver* ("to boil"). It is said that the sound of the frevo will make listeners and dancers feel as if they are boiling on the ground. Originating in 1909 when Zuzinha (Captain José Lourenco da Silva), director of the Pernambuco Military Brigade band, increased the tempo of the traditional polka-march. It began to be played in clubs in Recife during carnival in 1917.

marcha rancho: A genre developed in the middle of the 19th century that was influenced by Portuguese theatrical companies, which brought many marches to Rio de Janeiro in the 19th century. The name is derived from the "ranchos" (street carnival groups). The style uses binary meter, slow tempos, and includes elaborate and long melodic phrases. Lyrics are nostalgic and sentimental. Some examples of marcha rancho composers are Lamartine Babo, João de Barros (Braguinha) Ze-Keti, Max Nunes e Laercio Alves.

pandeiro: A handheld frame drum with a natural skin head and a series of bell-like cups embedded into the wooden frame. It is similar to the tambourine. The pandeiro is commonly found in many different types of Brazilian music, especially in *samba* and *choro.*

samba: The style generally considered to be the most characteristic and representative of Brazilian music. It had several influences, including lundu, la habanera, the maxixe, and even tango—bits of which remain in its unique sound. It has a definitive binary meter and is highly syncopated. Traditionally, the samba is played by strings (*cavaquinho* and various types of guitar) and various percussion instruments such as tamborim, caixa, *surdo,* among others. The most important samba compositions date from the 1920s to 1950 and include Jose Barbosa da Silva "Sinho," Noel Rosa, Alfredo da Rocha Viana "Pixinguinha," Ari Barroso, Lamartine Babo, João de Barros, and Ataulfo Alves.

samba partido alto: Refers to a type of samba with a number of particularities. In the world of samba subgenres and in samba reunions, partido alto songs (informally called "partidos") can represent a time for improvisation and (humorous or not) disputes, as well as a strong sing-along opportunity for the participants. In music theory, partido alto is also the name of a particular rhythm that is derived from the above-mentioned style of samba (especially in a jazz context). The rhythm is often played in samba, and is also the basis for the partido alto groove, in which more or all of the instruments accent this rhythm.

samba rock: This variation of samba is accredited to Jorge Benjor, the first person that was able to successfully bring the diverse styles together into a coherent, identifiable sound with his first recordings in the 1960s and '70s, including the first use of the electric guitar in samba. Unlike every other samba variation, this is to be played with a pick.

samba-bossa nova: A soft variation of samba that uses more complex harmonies and melodies.

sanfona: A Brazilian diatonic button-accordion (also called "acordeão"), typical of the Sertão region. It comes from European tradition, introduced to southern Brazil by Italian immigrants, and plays solo parts and accompaniment in different styles of music in the Northeast and South. There are many different types of sanfona, ranging from versions with only eight basses, to more technically developed ones.

surdo: A deep, double-headed bass drum used in various Brazilian styles. It most commonly includes a velvet-covered wooden head and is beaten with a soft mallet and an open hand. There are three types of surdos: the "marking surdo," which plays the heaviest form on beat 2 of a 2/4 *samba,* the "answering surdo," which plays less forcefully on beat one, and the "cutting surdo," which is the smallest bass drum that plays on the offbeats.

xote: Northeastern Brazil version of "schottische" (a kind of slower polka, with continental European origin) from which *forró* derived.

zabumba: A bass drum from Northeast Brazil, either 16 or 18 inches long, made with animal or synthetic heads. The top side, which is slightly thicker, is played with a mallet, and the bottom is played with a bamboo or plastic stick called the "bacalhau." The zabumba is worn by a strap in the front, on or above the drummer's waistline, in a diagonal fashion. Open and closed (muffling) strokes are both often heard.

HAL LEONARD GUITAR METHOD

by Will Schmid and Greg Koch

THE HAL LEONARD GUITAR METHOD is designed for anyone just learning to play acoustic or electric guitar. It is based on years of teaching guitar students of all ages, and it also reflects some of the best guitar teaching ideas from around the world. This comprehensive method includes: A learning sequence carefully paced with clear instructions; popular songs which increase the incentive to learn to play; versatility – can be used as self-instruction or with a teacher; audio accompaniments so that students have fun and sound great while practicing.

BOOK 1
00699010	Book	$8.99
00699027	Book with audio on CD & Online	$12.99
00155480	Deluxe Beginner Pack (Book/DVD/CD/Online Audio & Video/Poster)	$19.99

BOOK 2
00699020	Book	$8.99
00697313	Book/Online Audio	$12.99

BOOK 3
00699030	Book	$8.99
00697316	Book/Online Audio	$12.99

COMPOSITE
Books 1, 2, and 3 bound together in an easy-to-use spiral binding.
00699040	Books Only	$16.99
00697342	Book/Online Audio	$24.99

DVD
FOR THE BEGINNING ELECTRIC OR ACOUSTIC GUITARIST
00697318	DVD	$19.99
00697341	Book/CD Pack and DVD	$24.99

GUITAR FOR KIDS
A BEGINNER'S GUIDE WITH STEP-BY-STEP INSTRUCTION FOR ACOUSTIC AND ELECTRIC GUITAR
by Bob Morris and Jeff Schroedl
00865003	Book 1 – Book/Online Audio	$12.99
00697402	Songbook Book/Online Audio	$9.99
00128437	Book 2 – Book/Online Audio	$12.99

SONGBOOKS

ASY POP MELODIES
0697281	Book	$6.99
0697440	Book/Online Audio	$14.99

ORE EASY POP MELODIES
0697280	Book	$6.99
0697269	Book/Online Audio	$14.99

VEN MORE EASY POP MELODIES
0699154	Book	$6.99
0697439	Book/Online Audio	$14.99

ASY POP RHYTHMS
0697336	Book	$7.99
0697441	Book/Online Audio	$14.99

ORE EASY POP RHYTHMS
0697338	Book	$7.99
0697322	Book/Online Audio	$14.99

VEN MORE EASY POP RHYTHMS
0697340	Book	$7.99
0697323	Book/Online Audio	$14.99

ASY SOLO GUITAR PIECES
110407	Book	$9.99

ASY POP CHRISTMAS MELODIES
697417	Book	$7.99
697416	Book/Online Audio	$14.99

ASY POP CHRISTMAS RHYTHMS
278177	Book	$6.99
278175	Book/Online Audio	$14.99

AD LICKS
697345	Book/Online Audio	$10.99

HYTHM RIFFS
697346	Book/Online Audio	$10.99

STYLISTIC METHODS

ACOUSTIC GUITAR
00697347	Book/Online Audio	$17.99
00237969	Acoustic Guitar Songs (with Online Audio)	$16.99

BLUEGRASS GUITAR
00697405	Book/Online Audio	$16.99

BLUES GUITAR
00697326	Book/Online Audio	$16.99
00697385	Blues Guitar Songs (with Online Audio)	$14.99

BRAZILIAN GUITAR
00697415	Book/Online Audio	$14.99

CHRISTIAN GUITAR
00695947	Book/Online Audio	$16.99
00697408	Christian Guitar Songs	$14.99

CLASSICAL GUITAR
00697376	Book/Online Audio	$15.99
00697388	Classical Guitar Pieces	$9.99

COUNTRY GUITAR
00697337	Book/Online Audio	$22.99
00697400	Country Guitar Songs	$17.99

FINGERSTYLE GUITAR
00697378	Book/Online Audio	$19.99
00697432	Fingerstyle Guitar Songs (with Online Audio)	$14.99

FLAMENCO GUITAR
00697363	Book/Online Audio	$15.99

FOLK GUITAR
00697414	Book/Online Audio	$14.99

JAZZ GUITAR
00695359	Book/Online Audio	$19.99
00697386	Jazz Guitar Songs	$15.99

JAZZ-ROCK FUSION
00697387	Book/Online Audio	$22.99

ROCK GUITAR
00697319	Book/Online Audio	$16.99
00697383	Rock Guitar Songs	$14.95

ROCKABILLY GUITAR
00697407	Book/Online Audio	$16.99

R&B GUITAR
00697356	Book/CD Pack	$17.99
00697433	R&B Guitar Songs	$14.99

TENOR GUITAR
00148330	Book/Online Audio	$12.99

REFERENCE

ARPEGGIO FINDER
00697351	9" x 12" Edition	$7.99

INCREDIBLE CHORD FINDER
00697200	6" x 9" Edition	$6.99
00697208	9" x 12" Edition	$7.99

INCREDIBLE SCALE FINDER
00695568	6" x 9" Edition	$5.99
00695490	9" x 12" Edition	$6.99

GUITAR CHORD, SCALE & ARPEGGIO FINDER
00697410		$19.99

GUITAR SETUP & MAINTENANCE
00697427	6" x 9" Edition	$14.99
00697421	9" x 12" Edition	$12.99

GUITAR TECHNIQUES
00697389	Book/CD Pack	$14.99

GUITAR PRACTICE PLANNER
00697401		$5.99

MUSIC THEORY FOR GUITARISTS
00695790	Book/Online Audio	$19.99

www.halleonard.com

Prices, contents and availability subject to change without notice.

IMPROVE YOUR IMPROV
AND OTHER JAZZ TECHNIQUES WITH BOOKS FROM HAL LEONARD

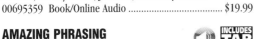

JAZZ GUITAR
HAL LEONARD GUITAR METHOD
by Jeff Schroedl

The Hal Leonard Jazz Guitar Method is your complete guide to learning jazz guitar. This book uses real jazz songs to teach the basics of accompanying and improvising jazz guitar in the style of Wes Montgomery, Joe Pass, Tal Farlow, Charlie Christian, Pat Martino, Barney Kessel, Jim Hall, and many others.
00695359 Book/Online Audio $19.99

AMAZING PHRASING
50 WAYS TO IMPROVE YOUR
IMPROVISATIONAL SKILLS • *by Tom Kolb*

This book explores all the main components necessary for crafting well-balanced rhythmic and melodic phrases. It also explains how these phrases are put together to form cohesive solos. Many styles are covered – rock, blues, jazz, fusion, country, Latin, funk and more – and all of the concepts are backed up with musical examples.
00695583 Book/Online Audio $19.99

BEST OF JAZZ GUITAR
by Wolf Marshall • Signature Licks

In this book/CD pack, Wolf Marshall provides a hands-on analysis of 10 of the most frequently played tunes in the jazz genre, as played by the leading guitarists of all time. Each selection includes technical analysis and performance notes, biographical sketches, and authentic matching audio with backing tracks.
00695586 Book/CD Pack... $24.95

CHORD-MELODY
PHRASES FOR GUITAR

by Ron Eschete • REH ProLessons Series

Expand your chord-melody chops with these outstanding jazz phrases! This book covers: chord substitutions, chromatic movements, contrary motion, pedal tones, inner-voice movements, reharmonization techniques, and much more. Includes standard notation and tab, and a CD.
00695628 Book/CD Pack... $17.99

CHORDS FOR JAZZ GUITAR
THE COMPLETE GUIDE TO COMPING,
CHORD MELODY AND CHORD SOLOING • *by Charlton Johnson*

This book/audio pack will teach you how to play jazz chords all over the fretboard in a variety of styles and progressions. It covers: voicings, progressions, jazz chord theory, comping, chord melody, chord soloing, voice leading and many more topics. The audio offers 98 full-band demo tracks. No tablature.
00695706 Book/Online Audio $19.95

FRETBOARD ROADMAPS –
JAZZ GUITAR
THE ESSENTIAL GUITAR PATTERNS
THAT ALL THE PROS KNOW AND USE • *by Fred Sokolow*

This book will get guitarists playing lead & rhythm anywhere on the fretboard, in any key! It teaches a variety of lead guitar styles using moveable patterns, double-note licks, sliding pentatonics and more, through easy-to-follow diagrams and instructions. The online audio includes 54 full-demo tracks.
00695354 Book/Online Audio $15.99

JAZZ IMPROVISATION FOR GUITAR
by Les Wise • REH ProLessons Series

This book/audio will allow you to make the transition from playing disjointed scales and arpeggios to playing melodic jazz solos that maintain continuity and interest for the listener. Topics covered include: tension and resolution, major scale, melodic minor scale, and harmonic minor scale patterns, common licks and substitution techniques, creating altered tension, and more! Features standard notation and tab, and online audio.
00695657 Book/Online Audio $17.99

JAZZ RHYTHM GUITAR
THE COMPLETE GUIDE
by Jack Grassel

This book/CD pack will help rhythm guitarists better understand: chord symbols and voicings, comping styles and patterns, equipment, accessories and set-up, the fingerboard, chord theory, and much more. The accompanying CD includes 74 full-band tracks.
00695654 Book/CD Pack.. $19.95

JAZZ SOLOS FOR GUITAR
LEAD GUITAR IN THE STYLES OF TAL FARLOW,
BARNEY KESSEL, WES MONTGOMERY, JOE PASS, JOHNNY SMITH
by Les Wise

Examine the solo concepts of the masters with this book including phrase-by-phrase performance notes, tips on arpeggio substitution, scale substitution, tension and resolution, jazz-blues, chord soloing, and more. The audio includes full demonstration and rhythm-only tracks.
00695447 Book/Online Audio $19.99

100 JAZZ LESSONS
Guitar Lesson Goldmine Series
by John Heussenstamm and Paul Silbergleit

Featuring 100 individual modules covering a giant array of topics, each lesson includes detailed instruction with playing examples presented in standard notation and tablature. You'll also get extremely useful tips, scale diagrams, and more to reinforce your learning experience, plus audio featuring performance demos of all the examples in the book!
00696454 Book/Online Audio $24.99

101 MUST-KNOW JAZZ LICKS
A QUICK, EASY REFERENCE GUIDE
FOR ALL GUITARISTS • *by Wolf Marshall*

Here are 101 definitive licks, plus demonstration audio, from every major jazz guitar style, neatly organized into easy-to-use categories. They're all here: swing and pre-bop, bebop, post-bop modern jazz, hard bop and cool jazz, modal jazz, soul jazz and postmodern jazz. Includes an introduction, tips, and a list of suggested recordings.
00695433 Book/Online Audio $17.99

SWING AND BIG BAND GUITAR
FOUR-TO-THE-BAR COMPING IN THE STYLE OF
FREDDIE GREEN • *by Charlton Johnson*

This unique package teaches the essentials of swing and big band styles, including chord voicings, inversions, substitutions; time and groove, reading charts, chord reduction, and expansion; sample songs, patterns, progressions, and exercises; chord reference library; and online audio with over 50 full-demo examples. Uses chord grids – no tablature.
00695147 Book/Online Audio $19.99

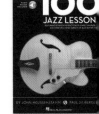

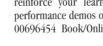

Visit Hal Leonard Online at **www.halleonard.com**

*Prices, contents and availability
subject to change without notice.*